Singing Bowls

Sound Healing Collection #1

Singing Bowls

A complete guide to singing bowls, covering their history, science, techniques, meditation and healing uses, and care.

Dharmapa

ISBN 978-607-99431-8-9

Table of Contents

Prologue   VII

Preface   XI

Chapter 1: Introduction to Singing Bowls   1

  1.1   Brief History and Origin of Singing Bowls   1

  1.2   Cultural and Spiritual Significance of Singing Bowls   5

  1.3   Types and Materials used in Making Singing Bowls   8

Chapter 2: The Science Behind Singing Bowls   13

  2.1   Exploration of the Physics and Acoustics   13

  2.2   How Singing Bowls Produce Sound Vibrations   17

  2.3   Sound Healing With Singing Bowls   21

Chapter 3: Types of Singing Bowls   25

  3.1   In-Depth Look at Different Types of Singing Bowls   25

  3.2   The Unique Qualities and Purposes of Each Type   28

  3.3   A Guide to Choosing the Right Singing Bowl   32

Chapter 4: PLAYING TECHNIQUES AND STYLES   37

   4.1 How to Play Singing Bowls Effectively   37

   4.2 Different Playing Techniques and Styles   43

   4.3 Tips for Creating Harmonious and
       Meditative Sounds   50

Chapter 5: SINGING BOWLS IN MEDITATION   57

   5.1 The Role of Singing Bowls in Meditation Practices   57

   5.2 Incorporating Singing Bowls into
       Mindfulness Routines   63

   5.3 7 Facts about the Benefits of Meditation
       on Human Health   70

Chapter 6: HEALING PROPERTIES   75

   6.1 Therapeutic Benefits of Singing Bowls   75

   6.2 Research on the Healing Effects of Sound Vibrations   78

   6.3 Practical Tips on Using Singing Bowls
       for Stress Reduction   80

Chapter 7: CARING FOR AND COLLECTING SINGING BOWLS   87

   7.1 Proper Maintenance and Care of Singing Bowls   87

   7.2 10 Points that Ensure a Long Life for
       your Tibetan Bowls   91

   7.3 Collecting Singing Bowls as Art and
       Cultural Artifacts   94

Prologue:

Dharmapa as a Master and Creator.

I still remember my first meeting with Dharmapa in a yoga center in Thamel, Kathmandu, Nepal. He was walking towards the center accompanied by his wife, Akbal. Right from the start, I sensed a powerful, pure and divine energy around him. During the past five years of knowing him, I have come to appreciate his unique gifts as a sound healer, spiritual teacher, and wonderful creator. He was born in Venezuela and learned his spiritual knowledge from his guru before moving to Mexico. There, he dedicated his time to working for humanity and teaching the wisdom of sound healing. Currently, for the past five years now, he resides in Nepal together with his wife, Akbal, who is a very esteemed feminine healer, a founder of a big feminine community "Shakti Healing System". Together, with their son, Shankar, they have been living in Nepal and working on spirituality.

What distinguishes Dharmapa as a sound healer is his unbelievable vocal quality. He is able to generate a variety of sounds with his voice that I have never heard in another sound healer. His whispering and vocal methods possess healing abilities which are simply incredible. He works in a special dimension, integrating his own creative sound healing instruments into his work.

A greatest asset of Dharmapa is his skill in making sound instruments. Not only is he an excellent healer but also a great craftsman. His productions include beautifully hand-crafted Jicuri Drums to handmade singing bowls, harps, and other ethnic instruments. It seems that there is no limit to his imagination—if he has the material to work with, he can produce any instrument. I once asked this of him, "Master, is it possible to create an instrument from a picture?" He simply replied, "I can create anything if I have the intention and the right materials."

His skill is marked by precision and depth of understanding regarding sound frequencies. He works with patience, calmness, and a strong sense of purpose, ensuring that each instrument has the right energy and harmony. From a Jicuri Drum to a singing bowl, every instrument he makes is perfectly balanced and energized.

Dharmapa also teaches the art of sound healing. Having been in one of his classes, I can confidently say that he is a great teacher—person who not only imparts technical knowledge but also an approach to life. He is humble, reflective, and patient in his teaching style. He also organizes spiritual retreats at "Busha Home," where he resides with his family. Being at the retreats has provided me with precious lessons in healing, personal growth, and self-awareness. His teachings encourage self-reflection—consciousness of our strengths and weaknesses and working on improving them with deliberate effort. Through his teachings, we learn to live simply and be satisfied with what we have.

Every time I hear the name Dharmapa, Akbal's name also crosses my mind. They are such a harmonious couple of masculine and feminine energy, giving a harmonious way of healing and spirituality.

I often reflect about Dharmapa's nature, ability, and perception, which seem to transcend the human experience. His wisdom and way of life resonates with the principles of Shiva.

In this book on singing bowls, Dharmapa shares extensive information about their significance, history, and application. Even those with no knowledge of singing bowls will gain deep insights from his first-hand experience. As he is among the manufacturers of these instruments, his understanding is first-hand. I recommend all the readers of this book to meet Dharmapa and at least try one of his courses to experience the energy in the field of healing and spirituality.

GOMA REGMI
Writer, Sound healer,
Shakti Healer & Astrologer

Preface

For over two decades, my journey has been immersed in the profound realm of sound healing, a global exploration that has unfolded across diverse corners of the world. My passion for this transformative practice has led me to a unique vantage point, currently residing in Nepal, where I dedicate my efforts to in-depth research on singing bowls and meditation techniques. This endeavor extends beyond scholarly pursuits to the creation of innovative musical and therapeutic instruments, coupled with the development of accessible methods that facilitate a clear understanding and seamless integration of sound healing into our spiritual lives.

My trajectory in the realm of sound healing has been a dynamic odyssey, fueled by a deep-seated curiosity and a commitment to unraveling the mysteries of sound and its impact on the human spirit. Having traversed varied landscapes and engaged with diverse cultural contexts, my experiences have shaped a comprehensive perspective that encompasses the rich tapestry of global sound healing practices.

Currently situated in Nepal, a land synonymous with spirituality and ancient wisdom, I find myself amidst a vibrant tapestry of traditions that have cultivated profound insights into the art of sound. The resonance of singing bowls, deeply embedded in the cultural fabric of Nepal, became a focal point for my research. It is within the serene landscapes of this Himalayan nation that I embark on a scholarly exploration, delving into the historical roots, cultural significance, and spiritual dimensions of singing bowls.

My research extends beyond a passive academic pursuit; it is a living, breathing engagement with the essence of sound. Nepal provides not only a geographical backdrop but a living laboratory where I immerse myself in the nuances of sound healing. This involves direct interactions with practitioners, yogis, lamas, artisans, and spiritual guides who impart invaluable knowledge and wisdom, contributing to a holistic understanding of sound's transformative potential. In the crucible of this immersive experience, I dedicate myself to the creation of new musical and therapeutic instruments. These instruments are not mere artifacts but embodiments of a profound understanding, crafted with intention and purpose. Each instrument carries the resonance of cultural insights, scientific knowledge, and a visionary approach to sound healing's applications in our spiritual lives. A pivotal aspect of my work involves developing methods that demystify sound healing and make it accessible to individuals from all walks of life. I recognize the significance of providing tools and techniques that transcend cultural and educational barriers, allowing everyone to harness the therapeutic power of sound in their spiritual journey. These methods are designed to be user-friendly, ensuring that the profound benefits of sound healing are within reach for individuals seeking to explore and enhance their spiritual well-being.

As a researcher, practitioner, and creator, my commitment extends beyond the academic realm to a broader vision of fostering a global community engaged in the transformative power of sound. The synthesis of ancient wisdom and contemporary insights, nurtured in the mystical landscapes of Nepal, shapes my endeavors to contribute to the evolving tapestry of sound healing. This journey is an ever-unfolding narrative, where the resonance of singing bowls becomes a symphony that echoes through the corridors of spiritual exploration and self-discovery.

May this book serve as a luminous beacon, guiding all who embark on the enchanting journey into the mesmerizing and potent universe of singing bowls. As you delve into the pages, may it unfold as a roadmap, illuminating the path towards a profound understanding of these ancient instruments and their transformative capabilities.

My deep gratitude to my beloved wife Akbal Sandoval Acosta and my son Shankar, who accompany me on this journey of self-knowledge and compassion. Namaste.

OM BUSHA HUM

Pharping, KTM, Nepal

2024

CHAPTER 1

INTRODUCTION TO SINGING BOWLS

1.1 Brief History and Origin of Singing Bowls.

Harmonic Resonance Through Time:
A Journey into the History and Origin of Singing Bowls

In the realm of ancient traditions and sacred practices, the resonance of singing bowls emerges as a timeless expression of harmony. This journey through the history and origin of singing bowls invites us to explore the cultural tapestry woven by these mesmerizing instruments, tracing their roots to the rich landscapes of Asia.

Ancient Beginnings

Singing bowls, also known as Himalayan bowls or Tibetan singing bowls, have a lineage that dates back over a thousand years. Originating in the Himalayan regions of Tibet, Nepal, India, and Bhutan, these bowls were initially crafted for ritualistic and spiritual purposes. Early artisans carefully combined a unique blend of metals, often including copper, tin, and other alloys, to create bowls with distinct tones and resonances.

Spiritual Significance

Embedded in the spiritual fabric of Tibetan Buddhism, singing bowls played a pivotal role in various ceremonies, meditation practices, and religious rituals. Monasteries and temples resonated with the deep, soothing tones of these bowls, believed to invoke a sense of tranquility and spiritual elevation. The sacred sound produced by the bowls was thought to aid in meditation, connecting practitioners with higher states of consciousness.

Cultural Evolution

As time unfolded, singing bowls transcended their religious origins and became integral to various aspects of Himalayan cultures. Their use expanded beyond monastic settings to include secular events, celebrations, and everyday life. The versatility of singing bowls allowed them to seamlessly integrate into the diverse cultural practices of the region.

Trade Routes and Global Influence

With the opening of ancient trade routes, particularly the Silk Road, singing bowls began to traverse continents, carrying with them the enchanting melodies of the East. The bowls found their way into the hearts of collectors, travelers, and seekers of spiritual enlightenment in the West. This global migration marked the beginning of a profound cross-cultural exchange, as the resonance of singing bowls echoed far beyond their Himalayan origins.

20th Century Resurgence

In the 20th century, singing bowls experienced a renaissance. As interest in Eastern philosophies and alternative healing practices grew, so did the demand for these mystical instruments. The resurgence of singing bowls paved the way for their integration into holistic wellness practices, sound therapy, and meditation techniques across the globe.

Modern Applications

Today, singing bowls continue to captivate individuals seeking balance and tranquility in a fast-paced world. From meditation studios to spa retreats, the harmonic vibrations of singing bowls are harnessed for their therapeutic properties. Modern practitioners and enthusiasts embrace these ancient instruments, recognizing their potential to facilitate relaxation, stress reduction, and a profound sense of well-being.

As we delve into the origins of singing bowls, we embark on a harmonious journey through time, bridging ancient traditions with contemporary applications. The echoes of these bowls resonate not only in the physical spaces where they are played but also in the collective consciousness of those who appreciate the enduring magic encapsulated within their metal alloys.

Seven key points when buying a singing bowl

1. Check tuning, use a digital tuner.

2. Identify if it is hand-made or by machine.

3. May the sound last a long time.

4. If it has symbols, know the meaning and what they are used for.

5. It should have an appropriate wood stick and cushion.

6. Check that there are no dents or cracks.

7. Confirm if it is a standard or full moon.

Later in this book, we will see these 7 points in detail.

1.2 Cultural and Spiritual Significance of Singing Bowls.

Rituals and Ceremonies

Singing bowls are woven into the cultural fabric of the Himalayan regions, where they play a pivotal role in religious rituals and ceremonies. In Tibetan Buddhism, for instance, the resonant tones of these bowls are considered sacred and are used to signal the beginning and end of meditation sessions, religious ceremonies, and rites.

The sound of the bowls is believed to purify the environment and create a sacred space for spiritual practices, fostering a connection between the earthly realm and the divine.

Communal Gatherings

Beyond religious contexts, singing bowls find their place in communal gatherings and celebrations. Whether it's a traditional festival in Nepal or a community event in Bhutan, the enchanting sounds of the bowls accompany cultural festivities. Their harmonious vibrations symbolize unity, shared experiences, and the interconnectedness of individuals within the community. Singing bowls, through their cultural resonance, become a symbol of cultural identity and shared heritage.

Meditation and Spiritual Exploration

At the heart of the spiritual significance of singing bowls lies their ability to facilitate meditation and spiritual exploration. The sound produced by these bowls is not merely an auditory experience; it serves as a medium to guide individuals into deeper states of meditation.

The resonant frequencies are thought to align with the vibrations of the universe, providing a conduit for spiritual seekers to access higher consciousness. In this way, singing bowls become tools for introspection, self-discovery, and the pursuit of inner peace.

Connection to Nature and the Cosmos

In many Himalayan cultures, there exists a profound connection between the natural world and spirituality. Singing bowls, with their metallic composition, are often seen as embodiments of the elements—earth, water, fire, air, and ether.

The act of playing a singing bowl is, therefore, a symbolic ritual that harmonizes the individual with the elemental forces of the universe.

The resonant tones are believed to echo the cosmic vibrations, creating a spiritual bridge between the human soul and the vastness of the cosmos.

Global Adoption and Integration

As singing bowls transcended geographical boundaries, their spiritual and cultural significance evolved. In the modern era, individuals from diverse cultural backgrounds have embraced singing bowls for their universal appeal and therapeutic qualities. The adoption of these bowls in global wellness practices has led to a fusion of cultural traditions, where the spiritual essence of the bowls resonates across continents.

Holistic Wellness and Healing

Singing bowls have found a home in the realm of holistic wellness. Beyond their cultural and spiritual roots, these bowls are now recognized for their therapeutic properties. Sound healing practitioners use singing bowls to promote physical, emotional, and spiritual well-being. The harmonious vibrations are believed to stimulate the body's natural healing processes, restore energy balance, and alleviate stress, fostering a sense of holistic wellness in individuals around the world.

In essence, the cultural and spiritual significance of singing bowls spans centuries, weaving through rituals, celebrations, and spiritual practices. As these sacred instruments continue to transcend cultural boundaries, they leave an indelible mark on the collective human experience, offering a harmonious bridge between the tangible and the transcendent.

1.3 Types and Materials used in Making Singing Bowls.

The Alloys of Melody

At the heart of crafting singing bowls lies the delicate art of alloy composition. Traditionally, singing bowls are made from a combination of metals, each contributing to the unique timbre and resonance of the final instrument. Copper, known for its malleability and sonorous properties, forms the backbone of many singing bowls.

Tin, another crucial component, enriches the alloy with its bright and clear tones. The proportion and combination of these metals, often accompanied by traces of other elements, create the alchemical blend that defines the voice of each bowl.

Traditional Materials and Techniques

Master artisans, following time-honored techniques, heat, shape, and hammer the metal alloys into the characteristic shape of singing bowls. The process requires a delicate balance of skill and intuition, as the craftsmen impart their energy into each strike of the hammer.

The resonance of the final bowl is said to carry the essence of the artisan's craftsmanship, creating a tangible link between the material world and the spiritual realm.

Tibetan Singing Bowls

Among the diverse family of singing bowls, Tibetan singing bowls hold a special place. Crafted by skilled artisans in the Himalayan region, these bowls are often characterized by a broader shape and a deep, grounding resonance.

The enigmatic tones produced by Tibetan singing bowls have been used for centuries in religious ceremonies, meditation, and spiritual practices. Each bowl, with its unique blend of metals and

craftsmanship, becomes a vessel for spiritual exploration and connection.

Crystal Singing Bowls

In contrast to their metal counterparts, crystal singing bowls are crafted from quartz crystal. Renowned for their clear and pure tones, these bowls are prized for their ethereal soundscapes.

The transparency of the crystal adds a visual dimension to the auditory experience, creating a captivating interplay of light and sound.

Crystal singing bowls are often associated with healing and meditation, as their tones are believed to resonate with the body's energy centers, promoting balance and well-being.

Himalayan Singing Bowls Beyond Tradition

While traditional Tibetan and Crystal singing bowls hold a timeless allure, modern innovations have given rise to a diverse array of singing bowls. Stainless steel, bronze, and even hybrid materials are now employed, expanding the sonic palette available to practitioners and collectors alike.

These contemporary bowls offer new possibilities for self-expression and exploration, blending the rich heritage of traditional craftsmanship with the spirit of innovation.

Selecting Your Sound Journey

As you embark on your journey with singing bowls, the selection process becomes a deeply personal exploration. Consider the intended use — whether for meditation, healing, or pure enjoyment.

Pay attention to the tone, resonance, and the visual aesthetics of each bowl. Whether you resonate with the ancient mystique of Tibetan singing bowls or the crystalline purity of crystal bowls, your chosen instrument becomes a companion on your path to sonic discovery.

In unraveling the artistry behind singing bowls, we delve into the alchemy of metal, the traditions of craftsmanship, and the diverse world of sounds these instruments offer. Each singing

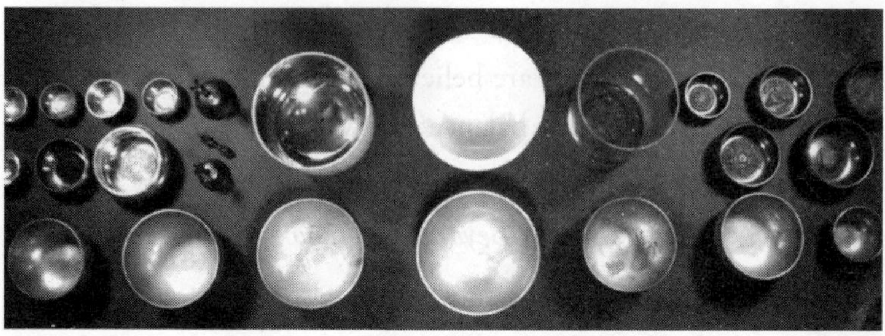

bowl, a testament to centuries of skill and culture, beckons you to explore the depths of its resonance and embark on a harmonious journey through the world of sound.

CHAPTER 2

THE SCIENCE BEHIND SINGING BOWLS

2.1 - Exploration Of The Physics And Acoustics

Vibrations in Metal

The essence of singing bowls lies in the physics of vibrations and resonance. When a singing bowl is played, it sets the metal into a state of vibration. This vibration, in turn, generates sound waves that travel through the air. The key to the unique quality of the sound produced lies in the composition of the metal and the shape of the bowl. The alloy's composition and the bowl's curvature determine the frequencies at which the metal vibrates, giving each bowl its distinctive voice.

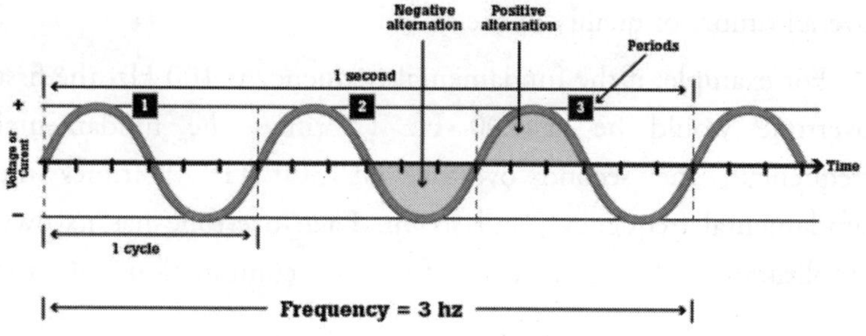

This distinctive voice is also known as pitch or frequency. Each bowl has its own tuning, which is measured in hertz (Hz), that is, how many times the bowl vibrates per second.

Standing Waves and Harmonics

As the singing bowl is played, it produces standing waves within its structure. These standing waves are the result of the constructive interference of the initial vibration and the reflected waves within the bowl.

The harmonics, or overtones, arise from these standing waves and contribute to the rich and complex sound profile of the singing bowl. The interplay of primary tones and harmonics creates the layered, ethereal quality that captivates listeners.

In the physics of sound, an overtone refers to a higher frequency component of a musical tone that is a whole number multiple of the fundamental frequency. The fundamental frequency is the lowest frequency at which a musical instrument or sound-producing object vibrates, determining the perceived pitch of the sound.

When a sound is produced, the vibrating object not only generates the fundamental frequency but also additional frequencies known as overtones or harmonics. These overtones are multiples of the fundamental frequency and contribute to the overall timbre or quality of the sound.

For example, if the fundamental frequency is 100 Hz, the first overtone would be at 200 Hz (2 times the fundamental frequency), the second overtone at 300 Hz (3 times the fundamental frequency), and so on. Each overtone has its own amplitude and frequency, and the combination of the fundamental frequency and its overtones creates the complex waveform that characterizes the sound of a musical instrument.

In the context of singing bowls, the overtones contribute to the rich and harmonic quality of the sound they produce. The interplay of the fundamental frequency and its overtones gives each singing bowl its unique and enchanting sonic signature. Understanding and manipulating these overtones are key aspects of the craftsmanship and playing techniques associated with singing bowls.

Sound Propagation

The physics of sound emission from a singing bowl involves the propagation of waves through the surrounding air. As the bowl vibrates, it pushes and pulls on the air molecules, creating compressions and rarefactions.

These pressure changes result in the formation of sound waves that travel through the air to reach our ears. The shape and size of the singing bowl influence the way these waves propagate, affecting the timbre and volume of the produced sound.

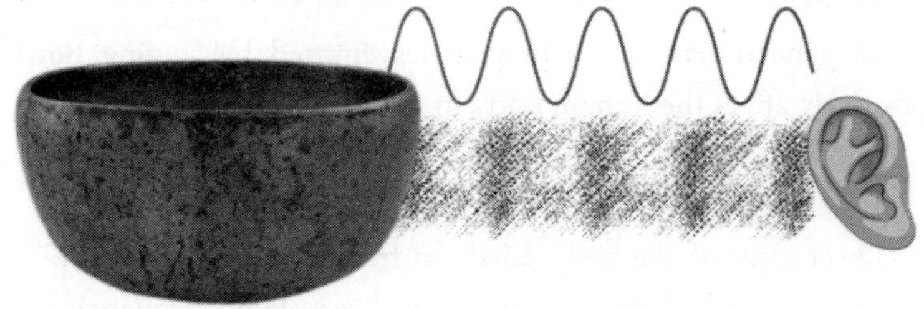

Resonance Frequencies and Harmonic Series

Resonance frequencies play a crucial role in the acoustics of singing bowls. These frequencies are determined by the size, shape, and material composition of the bowl. As the bowl is played, it naturally resonates at specific frequencies, creating a series of harmonics.

The harmonic series contributes to the richness of the sound, with each harmonic reinforcing the fundamental tone and adding complexity to the overall auditory experience.

Therapeutic Resonance

Beyond the aesthetic appreciation of their sound, the physics of singing bowls intersects with therapeutic applications. The vibrational frequencies produced by singing bowls are believed to have therapeutic effects on the human body. This concept aligns with the principles of vibrational medicine, where certain frequencies are thought to influence the body's energy centers, promoting relaxation, stress reduction, and overall well-being. The resonance of singing bowls becomes a therapeutic tool, engaging both the physical and energetic aspects of the listener.

In general terms, the frequencies emitted by singing bowls positively affect the human body in the following way:

Low frequencies *(between 27 and 216 Hz)*: Bones, tendons, lower areas of the body. Medium frequencies *(between 216 and 864 Hz)*: Thorax, solar plexus, heart. High frequencies *(from 864 Hz)*: Neck, face, brain.

Modern Innovations in Sound Healing

In the realm of modern sound healing practices, the physics of singing bowls has found new applications. Sound therapists and wellness practitioners harness the unique acoustics of singing bowls to create tailored experiences for individuals seeking healing and relaxation. The understanding of resonance frequencies, harmonics, and the psychoacoustic impact of sound allows for intentional soundscapes that support various therapeutic goals, from emotional release to physical rejuvenation.

In the exploration of the physics and acoustics of singing bowls, we uncover the intricate dance of vibrations, harmonics, and resonances that define these mystical instruments. From the ancient alchemy of metal forging to the therapeutic applications in contemporary sound healing, singing bowls stand as both a testament to the laws of physics and a source of transcendent sonic experiences.

2.2 How Singing Bowls Produce Sound Vibrations

The Initial Impetus

The journey of sound in a singing bowl begins with a simple yet profound action—a strike or a rub. When a singing bowl is struck with a mallet or played with a rubbing motion, it sets the entire

bowl into a state of vibration. This initial impetus imparts kinetic energy to the molecules within the metal structure of the bowl.

Vibrating Metal Alloys

Singing bowls are crafted from a specific blend of metals, typically including copper, tin, and other alloys. These metals are carefully chosen for their resonant properties. As the bowl vibrates, the metal alloys, bound by their inherent elasticity, respond to the kinetic energy by oscillating back and forth. This oscillation generates what is known as the f u n d a m e n t a l frequency—the lowest resonant frequency of the bowl.

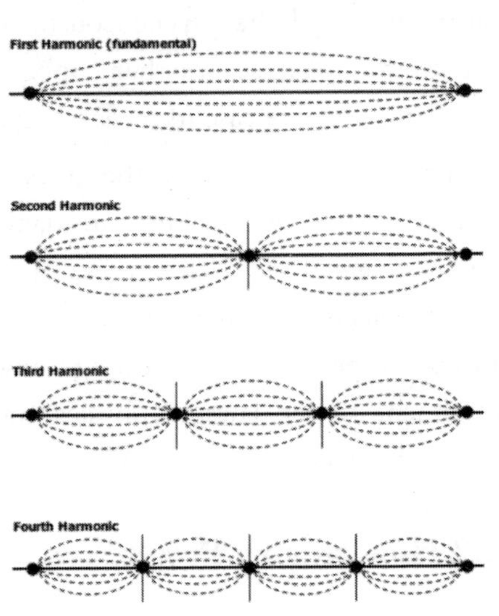

Resonance and Standing Waves

The vibrating metal of the singing bowl triggers a phenomenon known as resonance. Resonance occurs when the frequency of the external force (the strike or rub) matches the natural frequency of the bowl. The metal responds by absorbing and amplifying the energy at its natural frequency, causing it to vibrate with greater amplitude. This phenomenon is akin to pushing a swing at its natural frequency to make it swing higher and higher.

As the bowl continues to vibrate, it creates standing waves within its structure. These standing waves, characterized by regions of high and low pressure, become the building blocks of the bowl's sound profile. The first of these standing waves is the fundamental frequency, while subsequent waves are harmonics or overtones—multiples of the fundamental frequency.

Harmonic Series and Timbral Complexity

The harmonics, or overtones, add complexity and depth to the sound produced by the singing bowl. Each harmonic corresponds to a multiple of the fundamental frequency, and their combination creates a harmonic series. The harmonic series contributes to the timbre or quality of the sound, giving the singing bowl its distinctive and intricate sonic character. The interplay of the fundamental frequency and harmonics is what makes the sound of a singing bowl so enchanting and resonant.

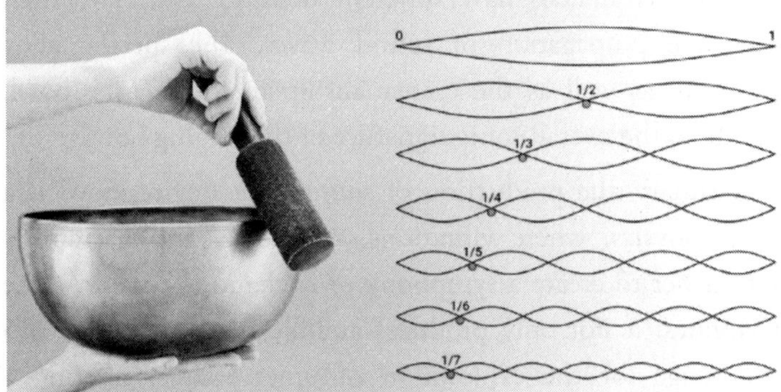

Influence of Bowl Shape

The shape of the singing bowl plays a crucial role in shaping the character of the sound produced. The curvature and thickness of the bowl determine the distribution of standing waves and, consequently, the frequencies at which the bowl resonates. Bowls with different shapes and sizes produce different sets of harmonics, contributing to the diversity of tones found among various singing bowls.

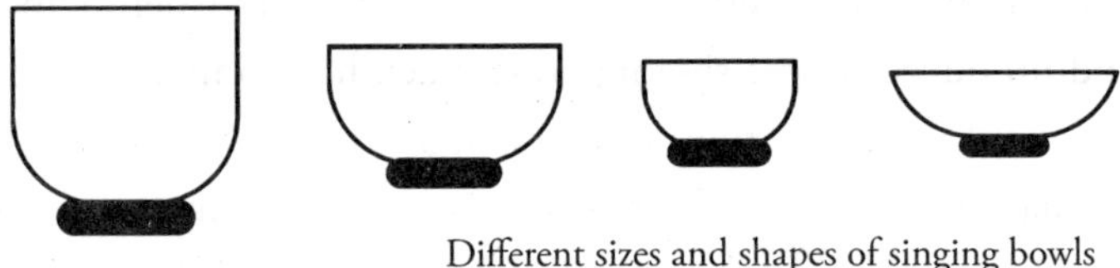

Different sizes and shapes of singing bowls

Material Composition

The material composition of the bowl, with its unique blend of metals, influences the speed at which sound travels through the metal. Different metals have different densities and elasticities, affecting the propagation of sound waves. The specific alloy composition, as well as the craftsmanship in forging the bowl, contribute to the overall sonic signature of the singing bowl.

In summary, the production of sound in a singing bowl is a dance of physics, where vibrations, resonance, and harmonics come together to create a symphony of enchanting tones. As the bowl vibrates, it not only produces audible frequencies but also sets the stage for the exploration of inner realms, offering a unique gateway to the harmonious interplay of physics and sonic beauty.

2.3 Sound Healing With Singing Bowls

Ancient Wisdom, Modern Applications

The therapeutic use of sound, particularly with singing bowls, draws upon ancient wisdom and healing practices. Rooted in traditions such as Tibetan Buddhism and Ayurveda, the belief in the profound impact of sound on the mind, body, and spirit has transcended centuries. In the modern era, the therapeutic aspects of sound healing have gained recognition, with singing bowls emerging as powerful tools for fostering well-being.

Resonance and Vibrational Medicine

At the core of sound healing with singing bowls lies the concept of resonance. The vibrational frequencies emitted by the bowls are thought to interact with the vibrational frequencies of the human body. This principle aligns with the foundations of vibrational medicine, which posits that different frequencies can influence the energetic balance within the body, promoting healing and restoring harmony.

Stress Reduction and Relaxation

One of the primary therapeutic benefits of sound healing with singing bowls is stress reduction. The calming and soothing tones produced by the bowls have a profound impact on the nervous system.

As the vibrations resonate through the body, they induce a relaxation response, lowering stress levels and promoting a sense of calm. This therapeutic effect is particularly valuable in today's fast-paced and often stressful lifestyles.

Balancing Energies and Chakras

In holistic traditions, it is believed that the human body has energy centers known as chakras. Each chakra is associated with specific frequencies, and imbalances in these frequencies can lead to physical or emotional distress. Sound healing with singing bowls aims to harmonize and balance these energies. Practitioners often use specific bowls corresponding to each chakra, allowing the vibrational frequencies to restore equilibrium and promote overall well-being.

Emotional Release and Mindfulness

The resonant frequencies of singing bowls can also facilitate emotional release and mindfulness. The immersive sound experience guides individuals into a state of focused awareness, making it an effective tool for meditation and self-reflection. The vibrations have the capacity to release blocked emotions, providing a cathartic experience and fostering a deeper connection to one's emotions and inner self.

Sound Baths and Group Healing

The communal experience of sound baths, where individuals gather to immerse themselves in the harmonious sounds of singing bowls, has gained popularity as a form of group healing. The collective resonance creates a shared space of tranquility and interconnectedness. Sound baths often incorporate various singing bowls, each contributing its unique frequencies to the collective therapeutic experience.

Integration into Clinical Settings

Beyond holistic and alternative practices, sound healing with singing bowls is making inroads into clinical settings. Therapists and healthcare practitioners are recognizing its potential as a complementary therapy for conditions such as anxiety, depression, and chronic pain. The non-invasive nature of sound healing makes it an appealing option for those seeking alternative approaches to well-being.

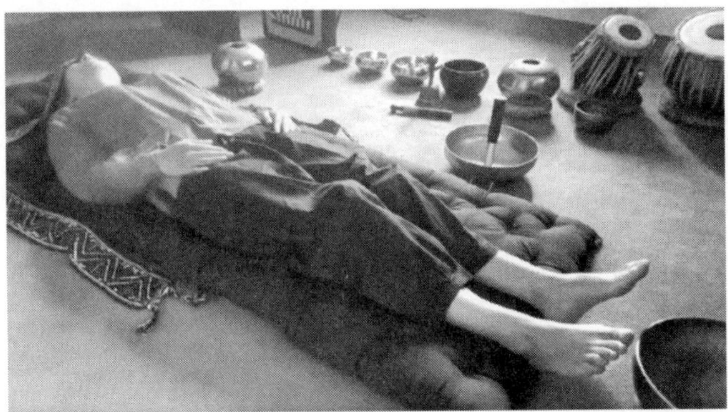

The therapeutic aspects of sound healing with singing bowls encompass a holistic approach to wellness, addressing the interconnectedness of mind, body, and spirit. As ancient wisdom converges with modern understanding, singing bowls emerge as not just instruments of beauty but also as catalysts for healing, offering a symphony of resonant frequencies that echo through the ages and into the hearts of those seeking therapeutic harmony.

CHAPTER 3

TYPES OF SINGING BOWLS

3.1 In-Depth Look at Different Types of Singing Bowls

Timeless Craftsmanship

Tibetan singing bowls, often referred to as Himalayan singing bowls, have a history deeply rooted in Tibetan Buddhist traditions. Crafted by skilled artisans in the Himalayan regions of Tibet, Nepal, Bhutan, and India, these bowls are renowned for their spiritual significance and traditional craftsmanship.

Typically made from a blend of metals, including copper, tin, and other alloys, Tibetan singing bowls exhibit a rich, grounding resonance that reflects centuries of cultural and spiritual heritage.

Characteristics and Uses

The distinct characteristics of Tibetan singing bowls include their wide, open shape and a fundamental frequency that resonates with a deep, soothing tone. These bowls are often used in meditation, prayer ceremonies, and rituals.

The harmonic overtones produced by Tibetan singing bowls are believed to aid in achieving states of deep meditation and spiritual connection. The art of playing Tibetan singing bowls involves techniques such as striking, rubbing, or even using a mallet to create intricate sounds that resonate through the bowl.

Transcendent Resonance

Crystal singing bowls, also known as crystal harps or quartz crystal bowls, offer a different sonic experience compared to their metal counterparts. Crafted from pure quartz crystal or a combination of quartz and other minerals, these bowls produce clear and pure tones.

The transparency of crystal allows for a visual and auditory journey as the light refracts through the bowl, enhancing the overall experience.

Healing Frequencies

Crystal singing bowls are celebrated for their association with healing frequencies. Each bowl is tuned to a specific note that corresponds to a chakra or energy center in the body.

When played, the pure tones are believed to resonate with these energy centers, promoting balance and clearing blockages.

The crystalline vibrations are thought to have a profound impact on the subtle energy system, making crystal singing bowls popular in sound healing practices and holistic wellness.

Stainless Steel, Bronze, and Hybrid Bowls

In the ever-evolving landscape of singing bowls, contemporary artisans and manufacturers explore diverse materials to create unique instruments. Stainless steel bowls offer a modern twist with their bright and resonant tones. Bronze bowls, while reminiscent of traditional Tibetan bowls, may incorporate innovative designs and shapes. Hybrid bowls may combine traditional metals with modern materials, showcasing the adaptability of singing bowl craftsmanship to new artistic expressions.

Selecting the Right Bowl for You

Choosing a singing bowl involves considering the intended use, personal preferences, and the sonic qualities that resonate with the individual. Whether drawn to the deep and grounding tones of Tibetan singing bowls, the crystalline clarity of crystal bowls, or the contemporary innovations in material and design, each type of singing bowl offers a unique sonic journey. Selecting the right bowl becomes a personal exploration, inviting individuals to connect with the instrument that harmonizes with their own vibrations.

The world of singing bowls is a symphony of diversity, weaving together ancient traditions, spiritual significance, and modern innovations. Whether crafted from metal or crystal, shaped in the traditional forms or pushing artistic boundaries, each singing bowl  type carries a distinct resonance that invites individuals into a sonic realm of beauty, spirituality, and therapeutic potential.

3.2 The Unique Qualities and Purposes of Each Type

Time-Honored Craftsmanship

Tibetan Singing Bowls, rooted in centuries of tradition, boast a unique blend of metals, including copper, tin, and various alloys. Crafted by skilled artisans in the Himalayan regions, these bowls are characterized by their wide, open shape and distinctive hand-hammered patterns.

The craftsmanship reflects a cultural and spiritual heritage, with each bowl telling a story of ancient wisdom and dedication to sacred artistry.

Sonic Tapestry

The unique qualities of Tibetan singing bowls lie in their harmonic richness and grounding resonance. The bowls produce deep, full-bodied tones that reverberate through the body and create a sonic tapestry of overtones. The combination of fundamental frequencies and harmonics fosters a meditative and introspective environment, making these bowls ideal for spiritual practices, meditation, and ceremonies.

Spiritual Significance

Tibetan singing bowls hold spiritual significance in Tibetan Buddhism, where they are used for meditation, prayer, and rituals.

The sound of these bowls is believed to carry healing vibrations that purify the environment and aid in spiritual elevation.

Beyond their ceremonial use, Tibetan singing bowls have found a place in the modern  world, embraced for their ability to promote relaxation, stress reduction, and a sense of connectedness to ancient spiritual traditions.

Purity of Sound

Crystal Singing Bowls embody a different sonic realm, crafted from pure quartz crystal or a combination of quartz and other minerals. Their unique quality lies in the purity and clarity of the sound they produce. Unlike their metal counterparts, crystal bowls create tones that are clear, bright, and resonate with a crystalline purity. The transparent nature of the crystal allows for a visual and auditory journey as the light refracts through the bowl.

Chakra Alignment and Healing Frequencies

Crystal singing bowls are often associated with energy work, chakra alignment, and vibrational healing. Each bowl is tuned to a specific musical note that corresponds to a chakra in the body. When played, the pure tones are believed to resonate with and balance these energy centers, promoting physical, emotional, and spiritual well-being. Crystal bowls have become integral tools in sound healing practices, where their clarity and precise frequencies contribute to therapeutic experiences.

Modern Aesthetics and Holistic Wellness

Beyond their traditional and spiritual roots, crystal singing bowls are favored for their modern aesthetics and adaptability to holistic wellness practices. Their resonance is embraced in yoga studios, meditation centers, and alternative therapy sessions. Crystal singing bowls offer an invitation to explore the intersection of ancient healing wisdom and contemporary well-being, making them sought-after instruments for those seeking a holistic approach to health.

Evolving Traditions

In the world of Modern Fusion Singing Bowls, craftsmanship takes on innovative forms. These bowls may be crafted from materials like stainless steel, bronze, or even hybrid compositions that blend traditional elements with modern aesthetics.

The unique quality of modern fusion bowls lies in their ability to bridge the gap between ancient traditions and contemporary artistic expressions.

Diverse Tones and Aesthetics

Modern fusion bowls offer a diverse range of tones and aesthetics. Stainless steel bowls may produce bright and resonant sounds, while bronze bowls may draw inspiration from traditional Tibetan designs while incorporating modern twists. The fusion of materials allows for a broad spectrum of sonic possibilities, appealing to those who appreciate both the roots of tradition and the evolution of craftsmanship.

Personal Exploration and Integration

Selecting a modern fusion bowl becomes a journey of personal exploration. These bowls cater to individuals seeking a synthesis of tradition and innovation, inviting a harmonious integration of the ancient and the contemporary. Whether used in meditation, sound baths, or as decorative elements, modern fusion singing bowls represent an evolving narrative in the world of sound healing.

In summary, each type of singing bowl, be it Tibetan, Crystal, or Modern Fusion, contributes a unique chapter to the symphony of sound exploration.

From the grounding resonance of tradition to the crystalline clarity of pure tones and the innovative fusion of materials, these bowls offer diverse qualities and purposes, inviting individuals into a rich and transformative sonic experience.

3.3 A Guide to Choosing the Right Singing Bowl

Understanding Your Purpose

When embarking on the journey to choose a singing bowl, it's essential to first clarify your purpose. Are you seeking a bowl for meditation, stress relief, energy healing, or as a decorative piece? Understanding your intention will guide you through the myriad options available and help you find the perfect bowl that resonates with your specific needs.

Tibetan Singing Bowls

If you are drawn to the rich cultural and spiritual heritage of Tibetan traditions, Tibetan singing bowls may be the ideal choice. Characterized by their grounding resonance and ancient craftsmanship, these bowls are well-suited for meditation, prayer, and spiritual ceremonies. Consider the size, shape, and tone of the bowl, as well as any unique markings or symbols that may hold significance for your spiritual practice.

There are basically 2 types of Tibetan singing bowls: those made by hand (*for healing purposes*), and those made by machine (*meditation and decorative purposes*).

Crystal Singing Bowls

For those seeking crystalline clarity and alignment with energy centers, crystal singing bowls are a compelling choice. Tuned to specific chakras and known for their pure tones, crystal bowls are suitable for energy work, sound healing, and creating a serene atmosphere. Explore the different sizes and notes available to find a crystal bowl that resonates with the specific chakras you wish to balance.

Remember the Seven key points when buying a singing bowl

1. Check tuning: use a digital tuner. You can use an app directly on your smartphone or a specialized tuner to tune instruments such as guitar, violin, etc.

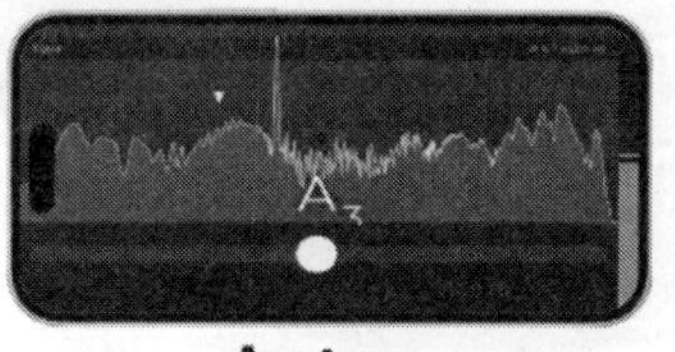

App tuner

Device tuner

2. Identify if it is hand-made or by machine. The machine-made bowls look with a perfect finish; the handmade ones look with traces or marks from the work done with a hammer; therefore, the finish is irregular and it shows that it is more artisanal.

Hand made   Machine made

3. May the sound last a long time. The resonance of the bowl depends on its materials and its dimensions. To verify this point, you can only rely on observation and listening to the bowl directly. When the bowl is made with 5 or more metals, its sound tends to last longer. The quality of the sound and its "sustain" varies considerably from bowl to bowl, so physically listening to it and comparing is the best option.

4. If it has symbols, know the meaning and what they are used for. There are 2 types of important decorations: painted and carved. When it is hand-carved the finish is much more beautiful and, of course, more expensive.

5. It should have an appropriate wood stick and cushion. The proper mallet should have one side of rough leather and the other side only of wood. Each area of this mallet produces different timbres when playing the bowl.

6. Check that there are no dents or cracks. If the bowl has been dropped or used roughly, it may break and generate unpleasant sounds. It can be repaired again, but the welding procedure will change its original sound.

7. Confirm if it is standard or full moon. Some artisans and manufacturers call full moon bowls those that were created during the night of the full moon. This procedure is believed to bring greater energy and power to the bowl. It is difficult to know if they were actually made during the night of the full moon; however, some have a special seal or mark that guarantees this procedure.

CHAPTER 4

PLAYING TECHNIQUES AND STYLES

4.1 How To Play Singing Bowls Effectively

Setting the Stage

Before diving into the intricacies of playing a singing bowl, create a conducive environment. Find a quiet and comfortable space, free from distractions. Place the singing bowl on a flat surface, ensuring stability. Consider sitting comfortably with a straight posture, allowing you to connect with the bowl effortlessly.

Choosing Your Mallet

Selecting the appropriate mallet is crucial for producing the desired sound. Mallets come in various sizes, materials, and

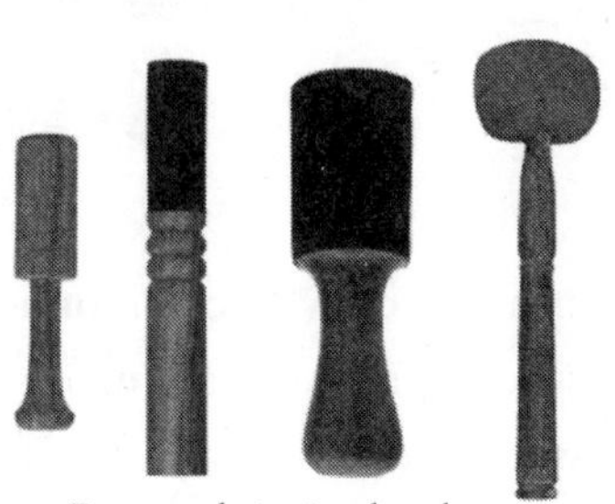

For metal singing bowls

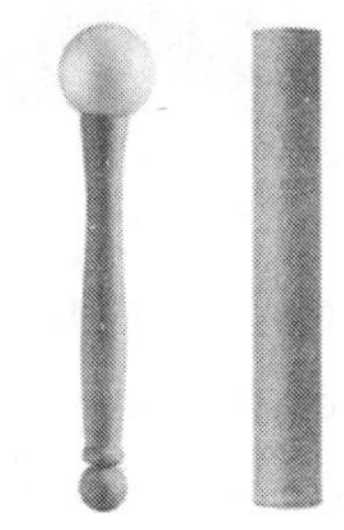

For crystal singing bowls

hardness. A soft mallet tends to create a warmer and gentler sound, while a harder mallet produces sharper and more pronounced tones.

Experiment with different mallets to discover the nuances each brings to the singing bowl.

Striking Techniques

There are two primary techniques for striking a singing bowl — the tap and the circle.

- **The Tap:** Gently tap the side of the bowl with the mallet to initiate vibrations. Allow the bowl to resonate, and pay attention to the subtleties in the sound. This technique is useful for creating a soft and introspective atmosphere.

- **The Circle:** With the mallet in hand, draw circles around the rim of the bowl. Apply consistent pressure and maintain a steady pace. The friction between the mallet and the bowl's rim produces a sustained sound. Experiment with the speed and pressure to find the sweet spot that elicits the desired resonance.

Finding the Fundamental Frequency

Every singing bowl has a fundamental frequency — the primary tone it naturally produces when played.

Experiment with different striking and circling techniques to identify the bowl's fundamental frequency. This foundational tone serves as a starting point for creating harmonics and exploring the bowl's full range of sounds.

When we play 2 or more bowls at the same time, it is important to know the laws of harmony, for example: if the bowl is tuned in C (Do), its best combinations would be with another bowl tuned in E (E) or G (G) .

Below I leave you 2 very basic harmonious combinations and their therapeutic effects:

Note 1	Note 2	Note 3	Effect
C	E	G	Balance & joy. This combination belongs to the C major scale which is very strongly associated with creating a happy mood.
C	Eb	G	Introspection, peace. This combination belongs to the C minor scale which is associated with a more melancholy feeling.

If you want to combine more than 3 bowls, do more research on scales, chords, and harmony for best results.

Playing with Pressure

The pressure applied during the circling technique significantly influences the sound produced. Light pressure results in a softer and subtler tone, while firm pressure yields a more pronounced and vibrant sound. Play with the pressure applied to the rim, and listen attentively to how it shapes the character of the sound.

Harmonizing with Overtones

As you circle the rim, listen for the emergence of overtones or harmonics. These higher-pitched tones accompany the fundamental frequency and contribute to the richness of the sound. Experiment with the speed, angle, and pressure of the mallet to coax out different harmonics. The harmonics add depth and complexity to the sonic experience of the singing bowl.

| On the tips of the fingers | On the palm | Palm and finger mute |

There are three basic ways to make the bowl sing: on the palm of your hand, on the tips of your fingers, and covering the bottom of the bowl with your hand and fingers. The palm and finger mute technique will help you hear the harmonics and higher sound of the bowl.

It is also important to regulate the speed of the circular movement and the amount of pressure exerted. Each bowl will teach you how to do it properly. It is a matter of practice and patience.

Intuitive Play and Mindfulness

Beyond structured techniques, allow yourself to play the singing bowl intuitively. Trust your instincts and let your connection with the bowl guide your movements. Play with mindfulness, focusing on the present moment and the sound unfolding. This approach encourages a deeper connection with the therapeutic and meditative aspects of the singing bowl.

Something that is very important is to keep your back straight when playing the bowl. Also, place it at the height of the center of your chest or in line with your heart. Another important tip is to smile and have your brow relaxed.

Combining Bowls for Harmonious Resonance

For those with multiple singing bowls, the art of combining them can create a harmonious symphony. Experiment with playing two or more bowls simultaneously, exploring the interplay of their frequencies. Consider the placement of the bowls and how their sounds complement and resonate with each other. This advanced technique requires practice and attunement to the unique qualities of each bowl.

Combining metal bowls and crystal bowls is very powerful; remember that in our blood we have minerals and metals. In fact, in order to activate our Kundalini, electromagnetism is essential, and this is increased with the resonance of the metal and crystal bowls wisely combined.

Incorporating Breath and Intention

Infuse your playing with intentional breath. As you play the singing bowl, synchronize your breath with the movements. Inhale as you prepare to strike or circle, and exhale as the sound unfolds. This mindful integration of breath enhances the meditative qualities of the practice and deepens your connection with the singing bowl.

As you have more practice, you will be able to synchronize the circular movement and your breathing in a rhythmic way; this will generate a much more powerful effect on your practice and on your audience.

Everything could be reduced to 3 aspects: technique, intuition, and mindfulness.

Technique: represents your masculine mind.

Intuition: your feminine mind.

Mindfulness: your presence, the balance between masculine and feminine.

As you see, playing singing bowls effectively is an art that combines technique, intuition, and mindfulness. From mastering the basics of striking and circling to exploring the nuances of pressure and harmonics, the journey of playing a singing bowl is a personal exploration.

Whether used for meditation, sound healing, or simple enjoyment, the effective playing of a singing bowl opens a doorway to a world of harmonious resonance and inner peace.

4.2 Different Playing Techniques and Styles

The Art of Striking

As I mentioned before, striking is one of the fundamental techniques for playing a singing bowl. Use a mallet to gently tap the outer edge of the bowl, initiating vibrations. This technique produces a soft and immediate sound. Experiment with different areas along the rim to discover variations in pitch and timbre. Striking is often an ideal technique for those seeking a quick and clear resonance. Also, try to hit the bowl aligned with your mouth half open so that your mouth space serves as a resonance box; you will notice that interesting sounds emerge. Use different types of mallets, materials, and sizes to find more resonance options. Example: wooden mallet, leather mallet, mallet with rubber head, mallet with cloth head, etc. I would only not recommend using a metal mallet to avoid an aggressive and uncomfortable sound.

The Dance of Circles

Circling is a more nuanced technique that involves continuous movement of the mallet around the edge. Start by applying even pressure and maintaining a constant speed. As you spin around the rim, the friction between the mallet and the bowl produces sustained vibrations, creating a fascinating, long-lasting sound. Spinning allows for greater control over the volume and intensity of the sound. You can also try to make a half circle continuously.

Combining Striking and Circling

Combining striking and circling is a dynamic approach that blends the immediacy of striking with the sustained quality of circling. Start with a gentle tap to set the bowl in motion and seamlessly transition into circling. This technique enables you to explore a spectrum of tones, from the initial strike to the ongoing resonance of circling. Mastering this combination adds depth and complexity to your playing style.

Harmonic Mastery

Harmonics are additional tones that accompany the fundamental frequency of the singing bowl. To explore harmonics, begin by circling the rim with consistent pressure. Gradually increase the speed, and listen for the emergence of higher-pitched tones. The mastery of harmonics allows you to create a multi-layered sonic experience, enhancing the richness and complexity of the sound.

Another effective way to highlight nuances is to apply the palm and finger muting technique. This specific technique requires practice and patience. To make it clearer, look at the image that I shared with you in the *"Harmonizing with Overtones"* section of this chapter.

Overtones - The Ethereal Symphony

Overtones are higher-frequency components that resonate above the fundamental tone. Experiment with various circling techniques to emphasize different overtones. Adjust the pressure, speed, and angle of the mallet to isolate specific harmonics.  Playing with overtones adds a transcendent quality to the sound, creating an ethereal symphony that captivates the listener.

Dynamic Range Exploration

Explore the dynamic range of the singing bowl by varying your playing techniques. Start with soft, gentle strikes and progress to more vigorous circling. Pay attention to the subtle shifts in volume, timbre, and resonance.

The dynamic range allows you to evoke different emotional and energetic responses, making your playing style more versatile and expressive.

Mindful Playing - A Meditation in Sound

Mindful playing involves approaching the singing bowl with focused awareness. Connect with your breath and intention as you play. Experiment with slow and deliberate movements, allowing the sound to unfold at its own pace. Mindful playing transforms the act of playing a singing bowl into a meditative practice, creating a harmonious connection between the player and the instrument.

Playing singing bowls is a meditation in itself and a very simple way to evoke higher states of consciousness.

Intuitive Exploration

Intuitive exploration invites you to let go of structured techniques and play the singing bowl based on intuition. Trust your instincts, allowing the sound to guide your movements. This style encourages a spontaneous and authentic connection with the bowl, fostering a unique and personal sonic expression. Intuitive playing is a gateway to discovering new and uncharted territories in the world of singing bowls.

The exploration of different playing techniques and styles for singing bowls offers a vast and transformative journey. From the fundamental techniques of striking and circling to the intricate realms of harmonics and overtones, each approach invites you to deepen your connection with these mystical instruments and unlock their full expressive potential.

Collaborative Playing

Consider collaborative playing by combining singing bowls with other instruments or playing alongside fellow musicians. Explore how the resonances of different instruments interweave and create harmonies.

Collaborative playing opens up possibilities for creating diverse and immersive soundscapes, making your singing bowl an integral part of larger musical ensembles or meditative gatherings.

Below I am going to leave you a list of instruments with which singing bowls combine perfectly.

Gongs

While singing bowls are characterized by their bowl-like shape and handcrafted designs, gongs are large, flat discs with a broad range of sizes and designs.

Both instruments, however, share the ability to produce mesmerizing sounds that resonate with individuals on physical, emotional, and spiritual levels. Whether used for meditation, therapeutic purposes, or musical expression, singing bowls and gongs continue to enchant and inspire people worldwide.

Tibetan Bells

Tibetan bells and singing bowls are selected to complement each other in terms of their pitch and resonance.

When struck or played together, these instruments create a harmonic synergy that enriches the overall sonic landscape.

Tingsha or cymbals

Tibetan Tingsha or cymbals are often used in combination with singing bowls to enhance the overall sonic experience during meditation, rituals, or sound healing sessions. During longer meditation sessions or sound baths, Tibetan Tingsha can be employed to mark transitions between different phases or activities. For example, a gentle ring of the cymbals may signal a shift from one meditation technique to another, creating a seamless and harmonious flow within the session.

Murchunga, jew harp

A Murchunga, also known as a Morchang, is a traditional percussion instrument from Nepal. It is a jaw harp, a musical instrument played by using the mouth to vibrate a reed or a metal or bamboo tongue. The 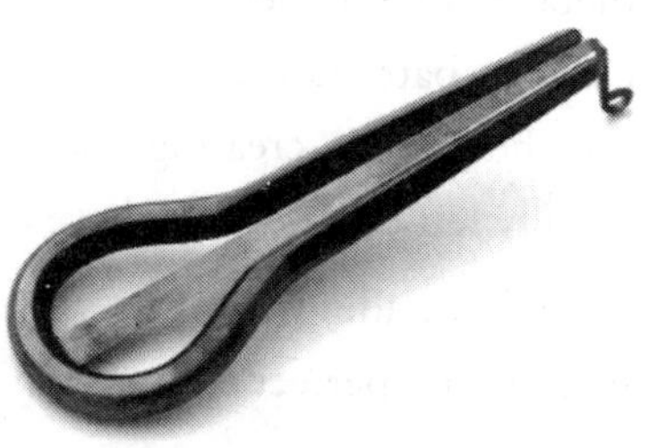 Murchunga specifically consists of a metal frame with a flexible metal or bamboo tongue attached to it. The player holds the frame against their teeth and plucks the tongue with their finger to produce sound.

Jicuri Drum or tongue drum

A Jicuri Drum, also known as a tongue drum, is a percussion instrument that belongs to the idiophone family. It is characterized by the presence of metal tongues or notes on its surface, which are played by striking them with hands or mallets to produce melodic and resonant tones. This instrument is very easy to play, produces soothing sounds, and is accessible in nature to both beginners and experienced musicians.

For more information visit: instagram.com/jicuridrum

A Jicuri Drum typically consists of a round or convex-shaped metal resonant shell with multiple tongues or notes arranged in a circular pattern on the top surface. The tongues are tuned to specific pitches, creating a scale or a mode. The top of the drum is usually left open or may have a hole to allow air to resonate.

It is made with the same materials as the singing bowls, making it a perfect companion when using Tibetan bowls.

4.3 Tips for Creating Harmonious and Meditative Sounds

Intention and Mindful Presence

Set Clear Intentions

- Begin your sound creation journey with a clear intention. Whether it's promoting relaxation, meditation, or healing, having a purpose behind your sounds helps guide your approach and energy.

Cultivate Mindful Presence:

- Engage in the process with full awareness. Be present in the moment, focusing on the sounds you're creating. Mindful presence enhances the quality of the vibrations and fosters a deeper connection with the harmonies.

Connect with Your Breath

- Sync your breath with the creation of sounds. Inhale and exhale with intention, allowing the natural rhythm of your breath to influence the pace and flow of the sounds you produce. This connection promotes a sense of calm and grounding.

Instrument Selection and Preparation

Choose Instruments Thoughtfully

- Select instruments that resonate with your intention. Whether it's singing bowls, Jicuri Drum, or other meditative instruments, each has its unique qualities. Experiment with combinations to find harmonious pairings.

Tune Instruments Mindfully:

- Ensure your instruments are properly tuned. Whether using singing bowls, tongue drums, or other tools, their harmonies should align with your desired atmosphere. Regularly check and adjust the tuning as needed.

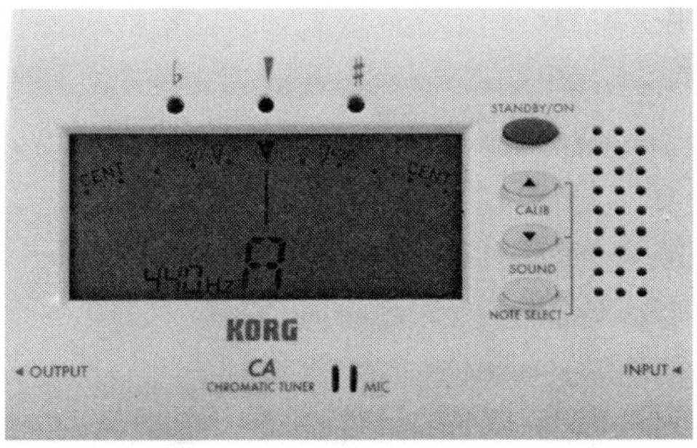

Create a Serene Environment

- Set up your space thoughtfully. Consider factors like lighting, room temperature, and comfortable seating. A serene environment enhances the overall meditative experience and allows the harmonious sounds to resonate more effectively.

Layering and Texture

Experiment with Layering

- Explore the rich tapestry of sound by layering different instruments or tones. Combine singing bowls with gentle bells or the soothing hum of a drone instrument. Layering creates depth and complexity in your soundscapes.

Balance Frequencies

- Pay attention to the frequencies of your instruments. Balance low, mid, and high frequencies to create a well-rounded and harmonious composition. Adjust the intensity of each element to achieve a balanced resonance.

Explore Textures and Timbres

- Embrace the diverse textures and timbres your instruments offer. Experiment with striking, rubbing, or bowing techniques to discover a range of sounds. The interplay of textures adds nuance and interest to your meditative sounds.

Mindful Playing Techniques

Practice Gentle Strikes

- When striking instruments, use a gentle touch. Whether it's a singing bowl, drum, or chime, allow the initial strike to be soft and deliberate. Gradually increase the intensity if needed, maintaining a mindful awareness of the vibrations.

Circular Movements

- Utilize circular movements when playing instruments with mallets or striking tools. This technique, especially with singing bowls, promotes sustained vibrations and a seamless flow of sound. Experiment with different speeds and pressures.

Explore Sustained Sounds

- Emphasize sustained sounds to extend the meditative experience. Whether through continuous bowing, holding a note, or allowing a singing bowl to resonate, prolonged sounds contribute to a calming and immersive sonic atmosphere.

Mind-Body Connection

Connect Emotionally with Sounds

- Infuse your sounds with emotion and intention. Connect with the vibrations on an emotional level, allowing your feelings to guide the creation of harmonious and meaningful sounds. Your emotional resonance will be felt by those experiencing the sounds.

Respond to Feedback

- Pay attention to the response of those engaging with your soundscapes. Adjust your techniques based on feedback, and be receptive to the ways in which your harmonious sounds impact others' well-being.

Working with symbols:

- Study the symbolism related to the presence of masculine and feminine energy in balance in order to use this knowledge for a guided meditation. The body is feminine, the mind is masculine.

Continuous Exploration and Refinement

Regularly Experiment and Refine

- Sound creation is an evolving practice. Regularly experiment with new instruments, techniques, and combinations. Refine your approach based on personal discoveries and the impact of your harmonious sounds on your audience.

Educate Yourself

- Invest time in learning about the instruments you use and the principles of sound therapy. Understanding the mechanics of harmonious sounds enhances your ability to craft intentional and effective sonic experiences.

Collaborate with Other Musicians

- Collaborate with fellow musicians or sound practitioners. Joint explorations can lead to unique harmonies and diverse perspectives, enriching your repertoire and introducing you to new techniques and instruments.

Explore the power of your voice

- Incorporate your voice by speaking softly or chanting some mantras that allow for a deeper spiritual connection.

The creation of harmonious and meditative sounds is an art that involves intention, mindfulness, and a continuous quest for sonic exploration. By incorporating these tips into your practice, you can refine your ability to craft resonant and immersive soundscapes that promote relaxation, meditation, and overall well-being.

CHAPTER 5

Singing Bowls in Meditation

5.1 The Role Of Singing Bowls In Meditation Practices

Introduction to Singing Bowls in Meditation

Ancient Roots and Spiritual Traditions

- Singing bowls have ancient origins rooted in spiritual practices, particularly in Tibetan and Himalayan cultures. They have been integral to meditation, prayer, and rituals for centuries, contributing to the creation of sacred and contemplative spaces.

Harmonious Resonance and Vibration

- The primary role of singing bowls in meditation lies in their ability to produce harmonious vibrations. The resonant tones emitted by the bowls serve as a focal point, guiding practitioners into a state of deep relaxation and heightened awareness.

Creating Sacred Soundscapes

- Singing bowls contribute to the creation of sacred soundscapes during meditation. The rich, enveloping tones help establish a tranquil and immersive environment, fostering an atmosphere conducive to introspection and inner exploration.

Establishing Mind-Body Connection

Balancing Energies

- The resonating sounds of singing bowls are believed to balance and align the energies within the body. The vibrations interact with the subtle energy centers, or chakras, promoting a sense of harmony and equilibrium. This balance contributes to a more centered and grounded meditation experience.

Mindfulness and Present-Moment Awareness

- Singing bowls serve as anchors for mindfulness. The sustained vibrations draw attention to the present moment, allowing practitioners to cultivate a heightened awareness of their breath, thoughts, and sensations. The mindfulness facilitated by singing bowls deepens the meditative experience.

Encouraging Deep Breathing

- The rhythmic and soothing sounds of singing bowls naturally synchronize with the breath. Incorporating deep, intentional breaths in harmony with the bowl's vibrations encourages a calming effect on the nervous system, fostering relaxation and stress reduction.

Sound as a Therapeutic Medium

Stress Reduction and Relaxation

- One of the key roles of singing bowls in meditation is their capacity to induce relaxation and reduce stress. The vibrations resonate through the body, releasing tension and promoting a tranquil state of mind. This makes them invaluable tools for stress management and overall well-being.

Sound Healing and Resonance Therapy

- Singing bowls are frequently used in sound healing practices. The therapeutic vibrations are believed to facilitate physical and emotional healing. The resonance therapy offered by singing bowls can address imbalances within the body and promote a sense of wholeness.

Enhanced Meditation Depth

- The unique tones of singing bowls can deepen the meditative experience. As practitioners attune themselves to the sound frequencies, they may access altered states of consciousness, experience inner stillness, and delve into the depths of their subconscious mind.

Guided Meditation and Visualization

Facilitating Guided Meditations

- Singing bowls serve as powerful tools for guided meditation sessions. Their resonant tones provide a gentle backdrop for guided visualizations, affirmations, or mindfulness exercises.

Journeying Within

- The immersive sounds of singing bowls invite practitioners on an inner journey. Whether exploring the landscapes of the mind or connecting with inner wisdom, the bowls serve as companions in the inward exploration, supporting a transformative and introspective meditation journey.

Varieties and Specializations

Diverse Types of Singing Bowls

- Singing bowls come in various types, each with its unique characteristics. Tibetan singing bowls, crystal bowls, Atlantis bowls, and other variations offer practitioners a spectrum of choices, allowing for personalized and specialized approaches to meditation based on individual preferences.

Atlantis singing bowl

Chakra Meditation and Alignment:

- Singing bowls are often aligned with specific chakras or energy centers. Chakra meditation, where each bowl corresponds to a particular chakra, aims to balance and align these energy points. This specialized use enhances the holistic nature of meditation practices, addressing both physical and energetic aspects.

Rituals and Ceremonial Practices

Ceremonial Beginnings and Endings

- Singing bowls play a ceremonial role in meditation practices, marking the beginning and end of sessions. Their resonant tones act as ritualistic bookends, signaling the transition into sacred space at the start and gently guiding practitioners back into the external world at the session's close.

Group Meditation Dynamics:

- In group meditation settings, singing bowls foster a collective and harmonious energy. The shared experience of resonant vibrations creates a unified field of consciousness, enhancing the interconnectedness of participants and contributing to a profound sense of unity.

Incorporation into Mindfulness Practices

- Mindfulness meditation benefits greatly from the integration of singing bowls. The synergy of mindfulness techniques with the harmonic frequencies of the bowls amplifies the effectiveness of cultivating awareness, presence, and non-judgmental observation.

Singing bowls play a multifaceted role in meditation practices.

From establishing a serene and mindful environment to offering therapeutic benefits and enhancing the depth of meditation, these ancient instruments continue to be cherished companions on the journey of self-discovery and inner peace.

5.2 Incorporating Singing Bowls into Mindfulness Routines

Introduction to Mindfulness with Singing Bowls

Mindfulness as a Path to Presence

- Mindfulness involves cultivating awareness of the present moment without judgment. Singing bowls, with their resonant tones, serve as anchors for mindfulness practices, guiding individuals into a state of focused attention on the here and now.

Singing Bowls as Mindful Anchors

- Utilize singing bowls as mindful anchors to bring attention to the present. The gentle and sustained tones of the bowls act as focal points, helping individuals redirect their thoughts away from distractions and into the current moment.

Setting the Intention

Begin each mindfulness routine with a clear intention. Whether it's cultivating inner calm, reducing stress, or fostering greater self-awareness, clarifying the purpose sets the tone for the mindfulness journey with singing bowls.

Establishing Mindful Breath Awareness

Breath Awareness with Sound

- Integrate singing bowls with mindful breathing exercises. As the bowls resonate, synchronize the breath with the rise and fall of the sound. This synergy enhances the depth of breath awareness, promoting relaxation and presence.

Guided Breathing Techniques

- Guide individuals through various breathing techniques using singing bowls. Incorporate techniques like deep belly breathing or rhythmic breathing, aligning each breath with the soothing vibrations of the bowls. This enhances the mind-body connection and promotes a sense of calm.

Mindful Listening Practices

- Develop mindful listening skills by focusing on the subtleties of the singing bowl's sound. Encourage individuals to observe the gradual onset, sustain, and fade of each tone, fostering a heightened sense of auditory awareness and concentration.

Body Scan Meditation with Singing Bowls

Body Scan Harmony:

- Introduce singing bowls into body scan meditations. As attention moves through different parts of the body, resonate the bowls to create a harmonious and immersive experience. This enhances the

mind's connection with bodily sensations and promotes relaxation.

Chakra Alignment with Singing Bowls

- Align singing bowls with the body's energy centers, or chakras, during mindfulness routines. Guide individuals through a chakra-focused meditation, using specific bowls to resonate with each energy center. This deepens the mind-body-spirit connection.

Chakra	Note	Color	Skill
Crown	B	Purple	Liberate
Third eye	A	Indigo	Visualize
Throat	G	Blue	Comunicate
Heart	F	Green	Feel
Solar plexus	E	Yellow	Express
Sacral	D	Orange	Create
Root	C	Red	Anchor

Sensory Awareness Integration

- Combine sensory awareness with the sounds of singing bowls. Encourage participants to explore various senses, such as touch, smell, and sight, while immersed in the resonant tones. This multi-sensory approach enriches the overall mindfulness experience.

Mindful Movement and Yoga Practices

Yoga Flow with Singing Bowls

- Integrate singing bowls into mindful movement practices, such as yoga flows. Align the tones with different yoga poses, transitions, or breath cycles. The synchronicity of movement and sound deepens the mind-body connection, fostering a meditative state.

Walking Meditation Harmony

- Extend mindfulness to walking meditations by incorporating singing bowls. As individuals take mindful steps, resonate the bowls at a gentle pace. This rhythmic integration enhances the awareness of each step and promotes a grounded and centered experience.

Transitioning with Singing Bowls

- Use singing bowls as transitional elements between different mindfulness activities. Whether moving from breath awareness to body scan or from sitting meditation to mindful movement, the bowls act as gentle guides, signaling smooth transitions.

Closing Mindfulness Routines with Singing Bowls

Reflective Sound Closure

- Conclude mindfulness routines with reflective moments accompanied by singing bowls. Allow the tones to gradually fade, providing a reflective space for individuals to absorb the benefits of the practice and transition back into daily life with a renewed sense of mindfulness.

Expressive Journaling

- Combine sound and expressive writing by incorporating journaling into the mindfulness routine. Invite participants to capture their experiences, emotions, and insights as they resonate with the lingering vibrations of the singing bowls. Journaling deepens self-reflection and mindfulness integration.

Mindfulness in Daily Life

Carry Mindfulness Beyond Sessions

- Encourage individuals to carry the essence of mindfulness with them throughout the day. Suggest using singing bowls as reminders for mindful pauses during daily activities. The simple act of striking a bowl can serve as a cue to return to the present moment.

Personalized Mindfulness Soundscapes

- Empower individuals to create their own mindfulness soundscapes with singing bowls. Offer guidance on selecting tones that resonate with their intentions and preferences. This personalized approach enhances the individual's connection with the practice.

Community Mindfulness Events

- Foster a sense of community by organizing group mindfulness events with singing bowls. Whether in-person or virtual, collective mindfulness practices with shared singing bowl resonances amplify the sense of interconnectedness and shared presence.

The integration of singing bowls into mindfulness routines adds depth, resonance, and a multisensory dimension to the practice. By weaving the harmonious sounds of singing bowls into various aspects of mindfulness, individuals can enhance their awareness, cultivate relaxation, and deepen their overall experience of being present in the moment.

Singing bowls offer profound benefits when incorporated into meditation practices, contributing to a heightened and transformative experience. These ancient instruments, with their resonant tones and harmonious vibrations, serve as powerful tools for individuals seeking deeper states of relaxation, focus, and inner exploration during meditation.

The primary benefit of singing bowls lies in their ability to induce a meditative state through sound. The rich, sustained tones produced by these bowls create a calming and immersive environment, acting as auditory anchors that guide practitioners into a state of profound relaxation. The gentle vibrations resonate through the body, promoting a sense of tranquility and reducing stress.

Moreover, singing bowls play a crucial role in establishing mindfulness during meditation. The sustained sound serves as a focal point, helping individuals anchor their attention to the present moment. By attuning to the auditory sensations of the bowls, practitioners can cultivate a heightened awareness of their breath, thoughts, and bodily sensations, fostering a deep sense of mindfulness.

The therapeutic aspects of singing bowls further enhance their benefits in meditation. The vibrational frequencies produced by the bowls are believed to promote physical and emotional healing. These therapeutic vibrations can resonate with and balance the body's energy centers, contributing to a harmonious flow of vital energy throughout the system.

Singing bowls also deepen the meditative experience by encouraging a mind-body connection. The resonance of the bowls synchronizes with the breath, promoting rhythmic and intentional breathing. This synchronization facilitates a state of coherence between the mind and body, fostering a sense of unity and interconnectedness.

Beyond their individual benefits, singing bowls can be incorporated into various meditation techniques. From guided meditations to body scans and chakra alignments, the versatile nature of singing bowls allows for a diverse range of meditation practices. Whether used in a group setting or during solitary meditation, the bowls create a sacred sonic space that supports individual journeys of self-discovery and inner peace.

The closing moments of meditation, accompanied by the gradual fading of singing bowl tones, provide a reflective space for practitioners to absorb the benefits of the practice. The transformative effects extend beyond the meditation session, influencing daily life by promoting a sense of calm, mindfulness, and overall well-being.

In essence, singing bowls enrich the meditative experience by creating a multisensory and therapeutic environment. Their harmonious vibrations guide individuals into states of deep relaxation, mindfulness, and inner exploration, making them invaluable companions on the journey of meditation and self-discovery.

5.3 Seven Scientific Facts about the Benefits of Meditation on Human Health

Meditation has gained increasing attention in scientific research, and numerous studies have explored its effects on human health. Here are seven scientific facts about the benefits of meditation:

1. Stress Reduction and Cortisol Levels

- Scientific studies consistently show that meditation can lead to significant reductions in stress. Meditation practices, such as mindfulness meditation, have been associated with lower levels of the stress hormone cortisol. Reduced cortisol levels contribute to a more relaxed state and are linked to improved overall well-being.

2. Brain Structure and Function

- Neuroimaging studies have demonstrated that meditation can induce structural changes in the brain. Regular meditation is associated with increases in gray matter density in areas related to memory, self-awareness, and compassion. Additionally, functional MRI (fMRI) studies indicate changes in brain activity patterns associated with improved attention, focus, and emotional regulation.

3. Mind-Body Connection

- Meditation has been shown to strengthen the mind-body connection. Research indicates that mindfulness meditation, in particular, can enhance awareness of bodily sensations and promote a more conscious relationship between the mind and body. This heightened awareness contributes to better stress management and a more holistic approach to health.

4. Immune System Function

- Scientific evidence suggests that meditation can positively influence immune system function. Meditation practices have been associated with increased activity of natural killer cells, which play a crucial role in the immune response. This suggests that regular meditation may contribute to enhanced immune function and better overall health.

5. Cardiovascular Health:

- Numerous studies support the idea that meditation positively impacts cardiovascular health. Meditation has been linked to reduced blood pressure, improved heart rate variability, and a decrease in the risk of heart disease. Mindfulness-based stress reduction (MBSR) programs, in particular, have shown benefits for individuals with hypertension and cardiovascular conditions.

6. Psychological Well-Being and Mental Health:

- Meditation is associated with various psychological benefits. Research indicates that regular meditation can reduce symptoms of anxiety and depression. Mindfulness-based interventions have been incorporated into clinical treatments for mental health disorders, demonstrating their efficacy in improving mood and emotional well-being.

7. Pain Perception and Management:

- Scientific studies have explored the impact of meditation on pain perception and management. Mindfulness meditation has been shown to reduce the subjective experience of pain and improve pain tolerance. Brain imaging studies reveal changes in neural pathways associated with pain processing, suggesting that meditation may alter the perception of pain at a neurological level.

These scientific facts highlight the diverse and well-documented benefits of meditation on human health.

From stress reduction and improved mental health to changes in brain structure and enhanced immune function, the scientific evidence supports the notion that incorporating meditation into one's routine can contribute to overall well-being and a healthier lifestyle.

CHAPTER 6

HEALING PROPERTIES

6.1 Therapeutic Benefits of Singing Bowls

The therapeutic benefits of singing bowls have been a subject of exploration, captivating the attention of researchers and practitioners alike. These ancient instruments, with their rich tones and vibrational qualities, offer a unique avenue for promoting healing and well-being. Here is an in-depth exploration of the therapeutic benefits of singing bowls:

Holistic Relaxation

Singing bowls are renowned for their ability to induce a state of deep relaxation. As the bowls are played, the resonant tones permeate the environment, creating a soothing sonic landscape. This auditory immersion has a profound impact on the nervous system, leading to a release of tension, reduction in stress levels, and an overall sense of tranquility.

Stress Reduction and Cortisol Regulation

Scientific studies have delved into the physiological effects of singing bowls on stress reduction. The vibrations produced by the

75

bowls have been linked to lower cortisol levels, the hormone associated with stress. This suggests that the therapeutic use of singing bowls can contribute to a hormonal balance that supports relaxation and stress resilience.

Mindfulness and Meditation Enhancement

Singing bowls serve as powerful tools for enhancing mindfulness and meditation practices. The sustained tones act as focal points, guiding individuals into a state of focused awareness. The rhythmic nature of playing the bowls can synchronize with breathing patterns, creating a meditative experience that deepens concentration and inner stillness.

Energy Balancing and Chakra Alignment

In holistic practices, singing bowls are often utilized for energy balancing and aligning the body's chakras. Each bowl is associated with specific frequencies that correspond to different energy centers. By playing bowls tuned to these frequencies, practitioners aim to restore balance to the body's subtle energy system, promoting overall well-being.

Sound Massage and Vibrational Healing:

Singing bowls are frequently employed in sound massage therapy, where the vibrations of the bowls are applied directly to the body. This form of vibrational healing is believed to stimulate cellular activity, promote circulation, and release energetic blockages. The gentle massage created by the bowls fosters a sense of relaxation and can contribute to physical and emotional healing.

Emotional Release and Catharsis

The therapeutic use of singing bowls extends to the realm of emotional well-being. The resonant frequencies generated by the bowls can facilitate emotional release and catharsis. The vibrations are thought to penetrate deeply into the emotional body, promoting a sense of clarity, release, and renewal.

Pain Management and Reduction

Research suggests that singing bowls may have analgesic effects, contributing to pain management. The vibrations can positively influence the perception of pain and potentially alleviate discomfort. Integrating singing bowls into pain management strategies offers a non-invasive and holistic approach to addressing physical discomfort.

Enhanced Quality of Sleep:

Singing bowls have been explored for their impact on sleep quality. The calming and harmonizing effects of the bowls can create an optimal pre-sleep environment, helping individuals

transition into a relaxed state conducive to restful sleep. This makes singing bowls a valuable tool for promoting better sleep hygiene and addressing sleep-related issues.

The therapeutic benefits of singing bowls span a wide spectrum, encompassing physical, emotional, and energetic dimensions.

From stress reduction and cortisol regulation to vibrational healing and emotional release, the exploration of singing bowls as therapeutic instruments reveals a holistic approach to well-being that resonates through the ages.

6.2 Overview of Studies and Research on the Healing Effects of Sound Vibrations

The exploration of the healing effects of sound vibrations has been a subject of growing interest and scientific inquiry. While the use of sound for therapeutic purposes dates back centuries, contemporary research has sought to unravel the mechanisms and benefits of harnessing sound vibrations for healing. This narrative delves into the studies and research that have contributed to our understanding of the profound impact of sound vibrations on human well-being.

Across diverse cultures and ancient traditions, the use of sound for healing has been a common thread. From the rhythmic drumming of indigenous tribes to the harmonic chants of Tibetan monks, the recognition of sound's potential to influence the human experience has persisted through time. Modern scientific exploration seeks to bridge the wisdom of these ancient practices with the rigor of contemporary research methods. One of the challenges in studying the healing effects of sound vibrations lies in quantifying the impact of frequencies that are often imperceptible to the human ear. Advanced technologies, such as spectrograms and oscilloscopes, enable researchers to visualize and measure sound waves with precision. These tools have become essential in unraveling the intricate patterns and frequencies that contribute to the therapeutic effects of sound.

Numerous studies have focused on the physiological responses triggered by exposure to specific sound vibrations. Research has demonstrated that sound can influence heart rate, blood pressure, and even the release of stress hormones. For instance, the gentle tones of singing bowls have been associated with a reduction in cortisol levels, highlighting the potential of sound to modulate the body's stress response.

The field of neurobiology has delved into the neurological impact of sound vibrations. Neuroimaging studies, including functional magnetic resonance imaging (fMRI) and electroencephalography (EEG), have provided insights into how the brain responds to different frequencies. Certain sound patterns have been linked to changes in brainwave activity, suggesting that sound vibrations may play a role in neuroplasticity and cognitive function.

At the cellular level, the concept of resonance takes center stage. Research has explored how sound vibrations can resonate with the cells of the body, influencing cellular activity and communication. This resonance is thought to create a harmonizing effect, potentially contributing to cellular repair and regeneration. Investigations in this realm aim to uncover the intricacies of the cellular dialogue facilitated by sound.

Psychoacoustics, the study of how the brain interprets sound, is a key avenue of research in understanding the healing effects of sound. Studies have investigated the psychological impact of immersive sound environments, exploring how specific sounds can induce states of relaxation, reduce anxiety, and enhance overall mood. This research has implications for designing therapeutic soundscapes in various settings, from healthcare facilities to wellness spaces.

In the realm of healthcare, studies have explored the clinical applications of sound therapy. Research within the field of integrative medicine has investigated how sound vibrations can complement conventional treatments. From pain management to mental health interventions, the integration of sound into healthcare practices is becoming a focal point for researchers seeking holistic approaches to well-being.

Despite the strides made in understanding the healing effects of sound vibrations, challenges persist. Standardizing study protocols, accounting for individual variations in response to sound, and navigating the interdisciplinary nature of this field pose ongoing challenges. The future holds promise for further exploration, with the potential for more robust clinical trials and a deeper understanding of the nuanced interactions between sound and the human body.

The studies and research on the healing effects of sound vibrations weave a tapestry that combines ancient wisdom with modern scientific inquiry. As our understanding evolves, the potential for sound to contribute to healing and well-being emerges as a fascinating frontier that transcends cultural boundaries and invites ongoing exploration and discovery.

6.3 Practical Tips on using Singing Bowls for Stress Reduction and Holistic Well-Being

Incorporating singing bowls into daily life can be a transformative and accessible way to manage stress and enhance overall well-being. Here are practical tips on using singing bowls for stress reduction and holistic wellness:

1. Establish a Ritual

- Designate a specific time each day for your singing bowl practice. Whether it's in the morning to set a positive tone for the day or in the evening to unwind, consistency enhances the ritualistic aspect and reinforces the benefits.

2. Create a Calm Environment

- Find a quiet and comfortable space where you can fully engage with the sounds of the singing bowl. Minimize external distractions, dim the lights, and create an environment that encourages relaxation and focus.

3. Mindful Breathing

- Begin your practice with a few minutes of mindful breathing. Inhale deeply, allowing the abdomen to expand, and exhale fully. Sync your breath with the gentle strikes or tones of the singing bowl, fostering a connection between your breath and the soothing vibrations.

4. Explore Different Techniques

- Experiment with various techniques for producing sound from the singing bowl. Whether using a mallet to strike the bowl, create a sustained tone by circling the rim, or experimenting with different playing techniques, each approach offers a unique sonic experience.

5. Intention Setting

- Before playing the singing bowl, set a positive intention for your practice. Whether it's to release stress, promote relaxation, or cultivate gratitude, framing your experience with intention adds depth to the therapeutic aspect of the sound.

6. Body Scan Meditation

- Combine the resonant tones of the singing bowl with a body scan meditation. As you play the bowl, bring your attention to different parts of your body, releasing tension and promoting a sense of grounding and relaxation.

7. Incorporate Visualizations

- Enhance your experience by incorporating visualizations. Imagine the vibrations of the singing bowl flowing through your body, clearing away stress and creating a harmonious balance within. Visualizations amplify the mind-body connection.

8. Personalize Your Practice:

- Each individual resonates differently with sound. Personalize your singing bowl practice by exploring different bowls, tones, and frequencies. Choose the ones that resonate most with you, creating a personalized and enjoyable experience.

9. Group Sessions

- Consider incorporating singing bowls into group sessions with friends or family. The collective resonance can enhance the sense of connection and shared relaxation. Encourage each participant to take turns playing the bowl, creating a collaborative and harmonious experience.

10. Sound Bath

- Treat yourself to a sound bath with multiple singing bowls. Place bowls around your space and play them in sequence, allowing the vibrations to envelop you. A sound bath provides a holistic experience, immersing you in a symphony of healing sounds.

11. Reflective Journaling

- After your singing bowl practice, take a few moments for reflective journaling. Capture your thoughts, emotions, and any insights that arose during the session. Journaling adds a contemplative layer to your practice, fostering self-awareness and growth.

12. Integrate Into Daily Activities

- Integrate singing bowls into daily activities. Play a bowl during moments of stress at work, incorporate it into your yoga routine, or use it as a prelude to bedtime for a restful night's sleep. Infusing these moments with the calming tones of a singing bowl can provide on-the-spot stress relief.

13. Learning and Exploration

- Invest time in learning about the art of playing singing bowls. Explore different playing techniques, understand the significance of various bowl types, and delve into the rich history and cultural contexts. Continuous learning deepens your connection with the practice.

14. Record Your Sessions:

- Record your singing bowl sessions to revisit and reflect on your experiences. The recordings serve as a personal archive of your journey, allowing you to track progress, notice patterns, and refine your practice over time.

15. Seek Guidance:

- If you're new to singing bowls, seek guidance from experienced practitioners or join a community that shares your interest. Workshops, online resources, and local gatherings provide opportunities to learn, share experiences, and refine your techniques.

Below are some of my online and in-person workshops:

ॐ Sound Healing Training:

Sound healing is a therapeutic practice that uses sound waves to promote physical and emotional healing. It involves the use of different types of sounds, such as singing bowls and drums, to produce vibrations that resonate throughout the body.

Sound healing is believed to work by stimulating the body's natural healing mechanisms, reducing stress and anxiety, and promoting a sense of relaxation and well-being. The practice has been used for centuries by different cultures around the world and is gaining popularity as a complementary therapy for various health conditions.

It can be done in a group setting or one-on-one with a practitioner, and each session is customized to the individual's needs.

What you will learn in this Training Course:

- The 3 systems of Sound Healing: Relaxation, Harmonization & Activation
- The use of rhythm in therapy
- How to use singing bowls to heal
- How to perform therapy with a Jicuri Drum

Other workshops available: How to create a Sound Journey. Rewire your brain with binaural beats. The ancient science of synchrobreathe. Initiation to Technoshamanism. For more information about my workshops, send me an email to: dharma_pa@hotmail.com

CHAPTER 7

CARING FOR AND COLLECTING SINGING BOWLS

7.1 Proper Maintenance and Care of Singing Bowls

Proper maintenance and care of singing bowls are essential to preserve their resonance, ensure longevity, and maintain their therapeutic qualities. Here's an in-depth exploration of the practices and considerations for keeping your singing bowls in optimal condition:

Understanding Your Singing Bowl

Before delving into maintenance practices, it's crucial to understand the composition of your singing bowl. Most traditional singing bowls are crafted from a blend of metals, often including copper, tin, zinc, and traces of other alloys. Additionally, crystal singing bowls are composed of quartz or other minerals. Understanding the materials will inform the appropriate care practices for your specific bowl.

Cleaning and Polishing

Regular cleaning is a fundamental aspect of maintaining the appearance and sound quality of your singing bowl. Use a soft, non-abrasive cloth to wipe away dust and residue after each use. For a more thorough cleaning, create a solution with warm water and mild soap. Gently clean the surface of the bowl, taking care not to use abrasive materials that may scratch or damage the metal or crystal.

Storage Considerations

Proper storage is crucial to prevent damage and maintain the integrity of your singing bowl. Store your bowl in a cool, dry place away from direct sunlight, as exposure to sunlight can lead to discoloration. Consider placing a soft cloth or cushion inside the bowl to prevent it from coming into contact with hard surfaces, minimizing the risk of scratches or dents.

Avoiding Extreme Temperatures

Singing bowls are sensitive to temperature variations. Avoid exposing your bowl to extreme heat or cold, as this can impact its structure and sound quality. Sudden temperature changes may cause the metal to expand or contract, affecting the bowl's resonance. If your bowl has been exposed to extreme temperatures, allow it to acclimate gradually to room temperature.

Handling with Care

When handling your singing bowl, do so with care and intention. Avoid gripping the bowl too tightly, as excessive pressure may alter its shape or affect the vibrations. Instead, cradle the bowl in your hand and allow it to resonate freely. Mindful handling not only ensures the longevity of the bowl but also contributes to the quality of the sound it produces.

Striking and Playing Techniques

Use appropriate striking implements, such as a padded mallet, to play your singing bowl. Striking the bowl too forcefully may not only produce an undesired sound but can also lead to structural damage. Experiment with different playing techniques to discover the nuances of your bowl's sound, but always approach the practice with a gentle and mindful touch.

Restoring and Tuning

Over time, the sound of your singing bowl may change or diminish. If this occurs, consider seeking the expertise of a skilled artisan or sound healer who specializes in the restoration and tuning of singing bowls. Professional care may involve adjusting the bowl's shape, refining the rim, or addressing any issues that affect its resonance.

Energetic Cleansing

In addition to physical maintenance, consider incorporating energetic cleansing practices into your routine. Some practitioners believe that singing bowls absorb and store energies from their surroundings. Energetic cleansing methods, such as smudging with sage or placing the bowl in moonlight, can be used to refresh and purify the vibrational qualities of the bowl.

Regular Playing Routine

Engage in a regular playing routine to keep your singing bowl in optimal condition. Regular use helps prevent stagnation and encourages the natural vibrations of the bowl. Even brief daily sessions contribute to the maintenance of its resonance and ensure that it continues to produce clear and harmonious tones.

Connecting with Your Singing Bowl

Caring for your singing bowl goes beyond physical maintenance; it involves forming a connection with the instrument. Take time to appreciate the unique qualities of your bowl, and approach each playing session with a sense of mindfulness and gratitude. This connection not only enhances your overall experience but also contributes to the energetic vitality of the bowl.

Community and Resources

Joining a community of singing bowl enthusiasts or seeking guidance from experienced practitioners can provide valuable insights into maintenance practices. Sharing experiences, tips, and recommendations within a community fosters a collective understanding of how to care for these unique instruments.

Conclusion

Proper maintenance and care of singing bowls are integral to preserving their beauty, resonance, and therapeutic qualities. By incorporating these practices into your routine, you not only extend the lifespan of your singing bowl but also deepen your connection with this ancient and powerful instrument.

7.2 10 Points that Ensure a Long Life for your Tibetan Bowls

Ensuring a long and vibrant life for your Tibetan singing bowls involves a combination of mindful practices and proper care. Here are ten points to consider that will contribute to the longevity and well-being of your Tibetan bowls:

1. Regular Playing Routine:

- Engage in a regular playing routine to prevent stagnation and keep the vibrations flowing. Regular use of your Tibetan bowl not only maintains its resonance but also prevents the accumulation of negative energies that may affect its vibrational qualities.

2. Mindful Handling:

- Handle your Tibetan bowl with care and intention. Avoid gripping it too tightly, as excessive pressure can alter its shape or affect the vibrations. Cradle the bowl gently in your hand, allowing it to resonate freely, fostering a mindful connection with the instrument.

3. Proper Striking Techniques

- Use appropriate striking implements, such as padded mallets, to play your Tibetan bowl. Avoid striking it too forcefully, as this may produce undesirable sounds and can lead to structural damage over time. Experiment with different striking techniques to discover the nuances of your bowl's sound.

4. Cleaning After Each Use

- Clean your Tibetan bowl after each use to remove dust and residue. Use a soft, non-abrasive cloth to wipe the surface, and if necessary, clean with a mild solution of warm water and gentle soap. Ensure the bowl is thoroughly dried to prevent water spots and maintain its appearance.

5. Storage in a Cool, Dry Place

- Store your Tibetan bowl in a cool, dry place away from direct sunlight. Exposure to sunlight can lead to fading or discoloration. Consider placing a soft cushion or cloth inside the bowl when storing to prevent direct contact with hard surfaces, minimizing the risk of scratches.

6. Avoiding Extreme Temperatures

- Protect your Tibetan bowl from extreme temperatures, as sudden changes can impact its structure and sound quality. Avoid placing the bowl in locations where it may be exposed to excessive heat or cold. Allow the bowl to acclimate gradually if it has been subjected to extreme temperatures.

7. Energetic Cleansing Practices

- Incorporate energetic cleansing practices to refresh and purify your Tibetan bowl. Some practitioners believe that singing bowls absorb and store energies from their surroundings. Methods such as smudging with sage or placing the bowl in moonlight can contribute to the energetic vitality of the instrument.

8. Mindful Storage

- When not in use, store your Tibetan bowl with mindful consideration. Avoid stacking heavy objects on top of the bowl, and use a padded carrying case if you need to transport it. Mindful storage practices protect the bowl from physical impact and potential damage.

9. Regular Inspection:

- Conduct regular visual inspections of your Tibetan bowl to check for any signs of wear or damage. Look for changes in its appearance, such as scratches or dents, and listen for alterations in its sound. Early identification of issues allows for prompt attention and preventive measures.

10. Seeking Professional Care

- If you notice significant changes in the sound or structure of your Tibetan bowl, consider seeking professional care. Skilled artisans or sound healers specializing in singing bowl maintenance can address concerns such as tuning, reshaping, or refinishing, ensuring the optimal performance and longevity of your bowl.

By integrating these ten points into your care routine, you not only contribute to the long life of your Tibetan singing bowls but also deepen your connection with these ancient and resonant instruments. As you engage in mindful practices and maintain a harmonious relationship with your Tibetan bowls, you become a custodian of their timeless tradition, ensuring they continue to inspire well-being for generations to come.

7.3 Information on Collecting and Appreciating Singing Bowls as Art and Cultural Artifacts

Collecting and appreciating singing bowls extends beyond the realm of music and sound therapy; it involves delving into the rich tapestry of art, culture, and history. Here is a comprehensive exploration of the facets involved in collecting and appreciating singing bowls as art and cultural artifacts.

Singing bowls, originating from diverse cultures such as Tibetan, Nepalese, and Japanese, are not merely musical instruments but embodiments of cultural heritage and craftsmanship. As collectors embark on this journey, they uncover a treasure trove of artistry, symbolism, and historical significance.

A crucial aspect of collecting singing bowls is delving into the cultural context from which each bowl emanates. Tibetan singing bowls, for example, are deeply rooted in Buddhist traditions and rituals. Understanding the symbolism and significance of these bowls within their cultural milieu enhances appreciation and adds layers of meaning to the collection.

Examining the materials and craftsmanship of singing bowls is integral to appreciation. Traditional bowls are often made from a blend of metals, each contributing to the unique resonance. The artisan's skill in shaping and crafting the bowl, along with any decorative elements, reflects the cultural aesthetics and technical mastery of the time.

Singing bowls carry a profound historical legacy. Collectors benefit from exploring the historical contexts in which these bowls were created. Understanding the periods, dynasties, or cultural movements during which certain types of bowls emerged enriches the narrative of the collection, connecting it to broader historical trajectories.

ॐ नमः शिवाय

Om Namah Shivaya

Many singing bowls are adorned with intricate symbols and iconography. These symbols, often drawn from religious or spiritual traditions, carry layers of meaning. Collectors may find joy in deciphering these symbols and appreciating the deeper significance embedded in the bowl's design.

The evolution of singing bowls over time reveals fascinating insights into cultural adaptations and influences. For instance, changes in design, materials, or the incorporation of new symbols may signify shifts in cultural dynamics, trade routes, or the assimilation of external influences.

Singing bowls exhibit remarkable diversity based on their geographical origins. Nepalese bowls, with their unique characteristics, may differ significantly from Japanese or Bhutanese bowls. Collectors immerse themselves in the geographical nuances, recognizing the distinct artistic expressions that emerge from various regions.

Ensuring the authenticity of a singing bowl is paramount for collectors. Provenance, or the documented history of ownership, adds value and legitimacy to a piece. Authenticating bowls often involves consulting experts, studying historical records, and, in some cases, relying on the oral traditions of the communities that produced them.

The patina that develops on singing bowls over time contributes to their aesthetic appeal. Collectors often appreciate the nuanced changes in color and texture, viewing them as a testament to the bowl's age and the journey it has undertaken through decades or even centuries.

Diversity in a singing bowl collection adds depth and breadth to the appreciation of these artifacts. Collectors may aspire to acquire bowls from different periods, regions, or cultural contexts, fostering a comprehensive understanding of the art form and its evolution.

As custodians of cultural artifacts, collectors play a crucial role in preservation and conservation. Implementing proper storage conditions, employing conservation techniques, and supporting ethical practices in the acquisition of singing bowls contribute to the longevity and sustainability of these cherished items.

Collectors often become ambassadors for the appreciation of singing bowls. Engaging with communities that produce these bowls, supporting local artisans, and sharing knowledge through educational initiatives contribute to the broader cultural awareness and conservation efforts.

Collecting and appreciating singing bowls as art and cultural artifacts transcend the boundaries of musical interest. It involves a holistic exploration of cultural narratives, craftsmanship, historical contexts, and the vibrant diversity embedded in these unique creations. As collectors immerse themselves in this multifaceted journey, they become storytellers, weaving together the threads of tradition, history, and artistic expression that resonate through each singing bowl in their collection.

ILLUSTRATIONS CREDITS

Every effort has been made to trace and acknowledge the original source of the illustrations used in this publication. We apologize for any omissions and will be pleased to make the necessary corrections in future editions.

1. Unknown

2. Instagram: @luckythanka. Thangka Painting | Buddhist Art for Mind, Body & Speech

3. shutterstock.com

4. cleanpng.com

5. Singing bowls set: https://www. himalayanbowls.com/

6. vecteezy.com: Metal Melting Videos.

7. freepik.com: PlaceboPill, Tibetan singing bowl.

8. flipkart.com: NA Feng Shui & Vastu Showpiece

9. soundwellness.com/bowls

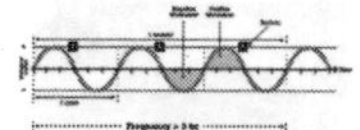

10. https://stackoverflow.com/ questions/23389972/why-bandwidth-is-measured-in-bits-per-second

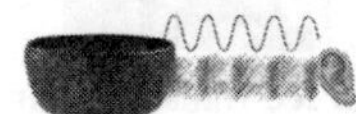

11. https://byjus.com/physics/speed-of-sound-propagation/

12. sciencephotogallery.com: Tibetan Singing Bowl #2 by Science Photo Library

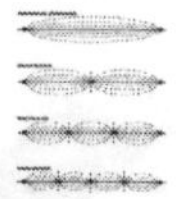

13. https://quizlet.com/201775114/ chapter-14-sound-waves-ï¬‚ash-cards/

14. https://concentricheal.xyz/services

15. Own design

16. Own design

17. Unknown

18. bushahome.com

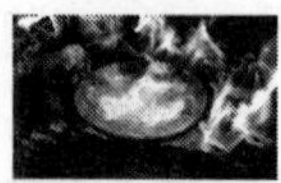

19. https://peace-trails.com/singing-made-singing-bowls/

20. Unknown

21. Unknown

22. Own design

23. mandalas.life

24. https://sunreed.com/

25. Own design

26. Unknown

27. eBay: sucille

28. Youtube: Himalayan Singing Bowl and trading

29. Unknown

30. yogaforharmony.co.uk

31. tching.com

32. Unknown

33. Photos & design by Dharmapa

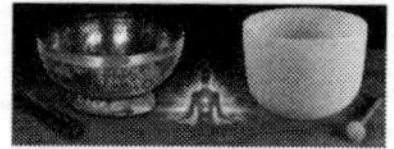

34. Unknown

35. Unknown

36. Unknown

37. Arborea gong

38. Unknown

39. Unknown

40. Unknown

41. instagram.com/jicuridrum

42. Unknown

43. https://concentricheal.xyz/services

44. Thamelmart

45. instagram.com/jicuridrum

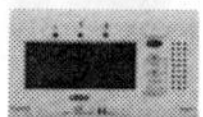

46. korg.com

47. bushahome.com

48. Unknown

49. Design by Dharmapa

50. Photos & design by Dharmapa

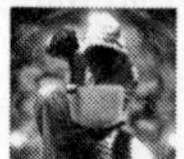

51. Photos & design by Dharmapa

52. Facebook: Mukesh Kumar

53. Unknown

54. https://www.rubenrobijn.nl/

55. Unknown

56. exportersindia.com: Divine Buddha

57. gettyimages.com

58. theohmstore.co

59. Unknown

60. yogazeit.com.au/the-power-of-the-singing-bowl/

61. mandalas.life

62. https://handicraftsinnepal.com/old-antique-tibetan-singing-bowl/

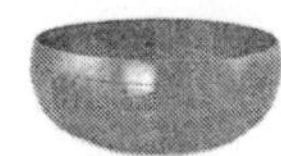

63. Unknown